A
WARRIOR'S GARDEN

*SEEDS OF A THERAPEUTIC APPROACH TO DEALING
WITH POST-TRAUMATIC STRESS DISORDER (PTSD)*

RALPH "MALACHIAS" GASKIN

A TRAITMARKER BOOK

Book Cover Design: Drew Macarthur
drewone.com

Author Photo Credit: Unnamed U.S. Army Specialist
Editor: Robbie Grayson
traitmarkerbooks.com

Cover Title Font, Headers & Text: Arial Narrow

Printed in the United States of America
Publisher: TRAITMARKER BOOKS
traitmarkerbooks.com
traitmarker@gmail.com

To order BULK copies, go to the BOOKSTORE page
at traitmarkerbooks.com

A truly inspiring and inspirational must-read that goes over the trials and tribulations involved with PTSD and soldiers returning home who are trying to adapt and find their inner peace. I am a firm believer that educating our troops is key so they can identify, seek treatment, and spread the word on how to tackle this demon. See, war is not a pretty thing, and each individual deals with it in his or her own way. Even though the topic is hard to digest, the book was an amazing wealth of knowledge. I hope that if any service member is in pain or knows of someone in pain, please, please, please, read A Warrior's Garden and seek out the proper treatment.

Ray Cash Care
Former Navy SEAL

5-STAR REVIEWS

Survivors know more than anyone what it feels like to be traumatized and live in the aftermath of uncontrollable emotional chaos, physical symptoms and mental interruptions. In the clutch of disconnection that post-traumatic stress creates most survivors have trouble finding the words to express what they feel, think and know -- but not Gaskin. From the very first page of this engrossing book Gaskin's conversational tone, honesty, creativity and diverse experiences offer not only an overview of how trauma affects a mind, body and soul, but also what it takes to heal. Reminding readers of the power of choice, action, self-advocacy, holistic approaches and partnership with the people who matter most in your life Gaskin paints a picture of both trauma and recovery that offers hope for survivors of any trauma. This book is like having a pal in your pocket gently reminding you that it is possible to access resilience and live again.

Michele Rosenthal
Founder, HealMyPTSD.com
Award-Nominated Author
Post-Trauma Coach
Radio Talk Show Host

For those that live with PTSD, for those that are the "Living Dead", and for those that care for them... This is likely one of the most important books you will ever read. It's not a clinical perspective, it's a real one. You can't read this book without shedding a tear and/or thinking, "Me too." I highly recommend it, and I believe it should be in every VA center, Military PX/BX and Library. M. Ralph Gaskin tells a story of solutions, healing and victory, not one of despair, sadness and defeat. If you want to understand, if you want to begin your journey to healing, read and practice what is in this book.

ECV
US Marine Warfighter

This book is not only showing the realness in PTSD and the struggles someone goes through, but Ralph helps you understand that you have to get out of the slump and take back control of you're life. I truly believe this book will be one for the ages to come. You will not only feel compassion and understanding, whoever reads this and truly digests the guidance that's presented within will forever be changed. A must-read!

J.H.
U.S. Army Music Composer

This book is a concise and informative read, yet truly inspiring. While the author suffers from PTSD, and has written this book to inform and help others in the same condition, I found that it serves as a great owner's manual for anyone whose brain has ever locked in on faulty thinking. It contains many concrete examples and useful suggestions about how to break out of the cycle, take ownership, and help yourself! As an aside, I love the cover art and will probably purchase a hard copy for that reason.

Mary K Rambinon

All of the solutions and guidance written in this book are well thought out and tested by a real hero suffering from PTSD. Through faith in God, love of country, family, and music, and a lot of experimentation, Ralph Gaskin has developed a routine that works well for him and could very well work for anyone suffering from PTSD. For anyone on the road to recovery, A Warriors Garden is a must-read. The simple, practical advice, and short, easy to read and understand chapters allow for a fast transition from the bondage of PTSD to freedom.

Iaian Thompson
U.S. Army Warfighter

I started reading, and I didn't want to stop. As a combat veteran, this book hits really close to home. Now, I don't have a garden, but as I read it I keep having the thoughts of how much it sounds like me, as if the words were taken from my life and someone else is telling my story. I'm only a few chapters in and have to force myself to stop reading because I don't ever want to come to the end of this book and it be over. I'm also thinking about starting a garden, then I go back and forth saying "Nah a garden is not my thing or is it? Nah, maybe?" The main focus isn't even about a garden! It's about us. The burnt-out combat veterans. We are not alone. Strength and Honor!

Jason T.

Strength and Honor

CONTENTS

DEDICATION

I dedicate my book to the following:
My Heavenly Father and Savior, Jesus Christ; my beautiful and supportive wife, Paige; my children, Brandon, Colin and Solaya; my parents who gave me life and raised me; and my sisters, Faith, Lynette and Gina.

ACKNOWLEDGEMENTS

I would like to thank the following people for inspiring me and for simply being a part of my life: Shawn and Holly Browning, Robbie and Sharilyn Grayson, Brett Manning, Iaian and Hannah Thompson, Shannon Marie Rafferty (for all of her proofing), and all the Soldiers with whom I have ever served!

INTRODUCTION

My name is Ralph "Malachias" Gaskin. I am a combat veteran of the Iraq war, having served in the Army for a combined 17 years and holding the military occupations of Infantryman and Medic. After two deployments I was diagnosed with PTSD. As I am writing this book, I am being processed for medical retirement due to my condition. I am in no way a medical doctor, psychologist or psychiatrist. I'm simply a Soldier who has tried as many things as possible to help me deal with my temper, and anxiety… my demons. This book is not designed to treat or diagnose any medical or psychological condition. It is simply written to share what I have done to treat myself. There is no one specific treatment or cure-all for PTSD. Everyone reacts differently to medications, therapy and so on. I have undergone treatment for five years and am hoping to continue improving.

I have tried several different things during the last five years: medication, therapy, herbal tea, and an all-organic and gluten-free diet. Please, don't read this and think that I am seeking pity or having a poor-me day. I am hoping and praying that by sharing what I have done, it might inspire or help someone else to find options that will help them. For those of you who have never dealt with PTSD or who have never known someone who does, IT SUCKS! For those of us who struggle with it, some of us don't even realize that we have it. We are fighting an internal war that never seems to end. It's almost like we never came home. At least parts of us haven't.

Of all the things I have tried, only three things have really made a difference in the way that I cope: growing deeper in my walk with God, gardening and music. This book will mostly focus on these three topics. My prayer is that it at least helps one person.

1
MY STORY

If double his strength, divide him.
Sun Tzu

I grew up in Fort Wayne, Indiana. My family owned a landscaping company from the time I was ten-years-old until my father passed away in 2004. *Gaskin Lawn and Fertilizing* was one of the larger, locally-owned landscaping companies in the city (Fort Wayne is the second largest city in the state). From the time I was thirteen, I was a supervisor and responsible for hiring and sometimes firing employees. That's a lot of responsibility for a teenager.

In June of 1992 I decided to drop out of high school and go to work full time. I was already making 25k a year, and (to be honest) like most kids I thought I was smarter than my teachers anyway. Kids, right? On January 4, 1994 I enlisted in the *Indiana Army National*

Guard and shipped to Fort Knox, Kentucky where I was the third generation in a row to attend basic training there. In September I attended AIT at Fort Sam Houston in San Antonio, Texas to become an Army Medic.

After I returned to Indiana I was assigned to Charlie Company 1-293rd Infantry as a Line Medic for an Infantry platoon. I was the only medic for the entire company for a year-and-a-half. I was very blessed to have been placed with some outstanding leaders. My First Platoon Sgt. was Staff Sgt. Charlie Cox. Charlie just retired as the State Command Sgt. Major.

Charlie took a lot of time mentoring me, and we became good friends. For the year-and-a-half, I was kept very busy as the only Medic. Charlie and I pretty much re-designed how Medics were utilized with the Infantry in the Guard. I honestly could not have asked for a better mentor! When the time came to stay as a Medic or change over to the Infantry, it wasn't really that hard. I stayed for a total of eight years and was promoted up to Staff Sgt.

In January of 2002, I was offered a Platoon Sgt. position in 113th Medical Support Battalion as the Treatment Platoon Sgt.: a no-brainer. It was my chance to be promoted to Sgt. First-Class and to have my own platoon to lead. Charlie and I discussed it for a few weeks, and he told me I would be stupid not to take it since I was ready. Isn't it great when someone you look up to and who has mentored you tells you that you are ready for the next step? It's amazing!

I took the position and led my platoon for one year when I finally decided that I was done and didn't feel like I wanted to make the Army a career anymore. I left the *Army National Guard* after nine years of service, and for the longest time I never thought twice about it. After my father passed away our family business was absorbed by the banks and lien-holders. It wasn't really a great feeling. For two years I struggled to find work. I didn't want to be a landscaper anymore, but landscaping and the Army was all that I knew. I was finally at a crossroads when my wife, Paige, and our three children were living in a single-wide trailer with my mother. I was working at a truck stop as a cashier for $6.75 an hour. Mind you, I was accustomed to making $18-$20 an hour. My wife and I discussed it, prayed about it, and I ended up back in the Army as a Medic stationed at Fort Stewart, Georgia.

From April 2006 to 2013 I have been active duty and have done several different jobs: Line Medic, Hospital Emergency Room NCO, Infantry Squad Leader and Army Bandsman. It has been interesting to say the least. After my first deployment to Iraq (for 15 months as a part of the Surge), I came home with a host of issues. Most of them I was clueless about. Not once during my childhood do I remember ever having a nightmare (that streak has long ended). For months I had serious issues with either falling asleep or suffering nightmares all night long.

I probably don't have to tell you that if you don't get a

good amount of sleep on a regular basis, it affects everything else about you like your mood, stamina, temper, weight control, general health and more. After having been home for five months, I couldn't understand why I was ticked off all the time. I would constantly yell at my children and wife who deserve better. I couldn't understand why I was so angry. Then came the internal struggle of knowing I shouldn't be that angry, and that caused me to be even angrier.

One evening in particular, we were at the dinner table. I couldn't stop yelling at my son. He became so upset that he started crying. That set me off! I started screaming to the point that my throat was killing me. I somehow managed to stand up and walk away into the garage. When my wife came out, I looked at her and said "Take me to the hospital. Something's wrong with me". At the hospital I was put on Seroquel for my sleep issues. Now, I'm not one of those guys who refuses to take medicine. If I have a headache, I have no problem taking some Motrin. But I am tired of being dependent on medication in order to sleep or not lose my temper. There has to be a better way! My wife and I started transitioning to an organic diet in 2011 which I believe has helped quite a bit. As an Army Medic, I understand that taking prescription medication on a long-term basis can have adverse effects.

That is the reason I am writing this book. I don't want to be tied to a medicine bottle for the rest of my life. There have to be alternative ways to treat it. You can't tell me that the Israelites didn't develop PTSD while enslaved by the Egyptians or from all the constant wars they had to secure the Promised Land. I'm sure they had PTSD, and without modern medicine I bet they had a way or found different ways to treat it. That's what this book is about: my journey as a Soldier to reduce my anxiety, help my sleeping, control my anger, and live a normal life.

I know that Soldiers are not the only ones who have to deal with PTSD. Anyone can develop it after a traumatic event. A severe car accident, being mugged, seeing someone get killed or die, being physically abused, or watching it happen to someone else can all cause PTSD. I have friends who have been gas station attendants for years, have been robbed, tied up, held hostage and more. They have the same issues that Soldiers do. I am writing this from the Soldier's standpoint because that is what I personally know. I'm not trying to downplay or negate the people who have never been in the military.

There are three things in my life that have helped me a great deal: music, gardening, and my faith in God. Now don't freak out. This isn't going to be a book that tries to convert you to Christianity. I am simply sharing what has helped me. Hopefully, you will find something in here that can help you on your journey.

2
MUSIC

It is the warrior's way to follow the paths of both the sword and brush [pen].
Musashi

I honestly can't get enough of music. I have been blessed for the last couple of years to be a Musician for the *U.S. Army*. I have been in and out of bands as a vocalist since 1992: punk, metal, hard rock... it really didn't matter. I just wanted to perform and sing. In 2007 during my first deployment I made a deal with my Chain-of-Command that I would re-enlist while in Iraq if I could be given the chance to audition with the Army Band. Seven months later, I finally got the chance. After we returned from the desert a few months later, I reported to the 3rd Infantry Division Band at Fort Stewart.

I deployed to Iraq again with the band and was blessed to finally be making music for a living. I love the fact that I am a Musician. I could not imagine doing anything else in the Army anymore. On my first deployment during the Surge in 2007-2008 I was a Medic for a Security Platoon, and I provided a security escort for an EOD team. That mission ended, and we were moved to provide assistance at a patrol base and to conduct village-cataloging and more. There, I was utilized in both infantry and medical capacities. I finished that deployment as the NCO in charge of a Level 2 Combat Support Hospital.

Aside from praying on a regular basis, music is a major part of what has helped me deal my PTSD. You will never see me without my laptop or MP3 player, listening to music all while dreaming up my own lyrics, getting back on stage and performing again. Of course, that dream was realized in October 2008 when I was moved to the 3ID band and shortly thereafter deployed again in 2009-2010 to provide musical support for Northern Iraq. We toured all over, playing for thousands upon thousands of Soldiers, civilians and local nationals. I was given the chance to be the hype man for *5 Finger Death Punch,* sing with *Finger 11,* and open up for *Vertical Horizon.*

Over the last two years I have been blessed to have vocal lessons with Brett Manning and Jason Catron of *Singing Success* and the company *Sing! Tenore.* I have no complaints about the life that God has blessed me with. There was a short while ago when I was talking to my buddy, Robbie Grayson, who was putting together a documentary with the help of the *Nashville Film Institute*

(NFI) and Prema Thiagarajah about how I used music as a coping method for my PTSD. Of course, being in the Army there are rules about how and when I can do certain things. So that part of my life has been on hold until after retirement. But I digress.

Over the last few years I have purged my music cataloged and removed a lot of music. To be honest, I removed anything that wasn't from a Christian artist. I'm not saying that has to be done. It was a personal choice, plain and simple. I did it for two reasons. First, I wanted to surround myself with positive and uplifting music. I'm not saying that my collection is exclusively all praise and worship music. In fact, I have a lot of metal, hard rock, pop and more. But they are not what others might consider to be mainstream music. You know what I am talking about: songs talking about going to the club, drinking, drugs and partying.

I am constantly listening to music, getting lost in it, and using it to inspire me to continue writing when I retire from the Army. Your mind like your body is what you put into it. If you fill your body with sugar, drugs and processed food, it will turn on you and break down. If you fill your mind with hateful, aggressive, and immoral things on a regular basis, it may only encourage you to sit and wallow in your pain and suffering.

You don't have to delete all your music and buy all Christian artists. That's not what I am suggesting. I'm suggesting that you sit back and think about what you are putting into your mind. You may surprise yourself with what is actually being processed. For example, when I get ticked off and need some hard music to help me let go of some aggression, I throw in some *Demon Hunter, Red, Since October, Disciple Grave Robber* and more. It's heavy music but not angry and detrimental. Again, this is just what I have done and has worked for me. If you don't sing or play an instrument of any kind, I highly suggest trying to learn. Take lessons and have fun with it. You never know what might happen!

Music is an outlet for the soul! It allows you to put into song what you are feeling or experiencing. It has been such an amazing type of self-therapy for me, and I suggest that everyone use some type of music in their lives... even if that just means throwing on some ear buds and vegging out. Since my first deployment, I have had a terrible time going out in public. We live on a military instillation which is connected to a small town. The "mall" here is Walmart... just saying! One of the things I have done that helps so much for me is to put my music player on my cell phone and play music while we walk through crowded stores. It is just enough to keep my peripheral thoughts and sights distracted so that I don't get overly anxious. I've noticed that since I have begun doing that, I have not been so agitated or anxious! I even did my own trial with it. I went on several shopping trips with my wife while having music on. I stayed relatively calm. On the contrary, when I didn't use the music I pretty much ruined most of our shopping trips.

At times surrounding myself with music irritates my wife. But she puts up with it for my sake. She is so amazing and such a trooper when dealing with me. I have been so blessed with a wife who is as patient and as understanding as she is. So let me just say "Thank you, Paige! I love you so much!" Let me also add that it does help that she loves music too. I do at times feel like I am spoiled.

This is how my listening method works. While the music is playing, it isn't so loud that it blocks everything out. It's loud enough that I can hear it, make out the words, and drown out the background noise to keep my anxiety down. When the music isn't playing, every little slam, bang, kid squealing... everything... quickly gets on my nerves and I get defensive. It reminds me of going through a small village on a patrol. You get confined in movement due to short walls and crowds... depending on the time of day. Then you throw in all the background noise of irrigation machines or animals and kids and, you just pray nothing is going to happen. It's bad enough that every aisle we go down makes me feel trapped, constricted, boxed in and choked. But when I have the music playing in the store with me, it helps me not to focus on all the distractions but on my wife, our conversation, our kids and shopping in general. I know it doesn't please everyone that I have the music playing in my ears, but without it I am liable to choke someone. (Not literally, but it could happen). So if you have any type of social anxiety, try this the next time you are out.

See if it helps you at all. For those of you who also want to try the creative part of music, it will be the best outlet you will ever try. I have written several songs that have specifically been nothing more than therapy for me.

I don't keep a journal. I write songs. I get my pain, my anguish, my memories, and my thoughts out and expressed that way. For some reason, I suck at simply talking things out at times. It feels so much easier to write lyrics to a song than to see a therapist. I know that therapists work for some people, but from personal experience, I never felt as though mine did anything other than listen and prescribe medication. I personally wanted and needed more. I don't want to have to take medications that have more side effects than I have hair on my head. Do they help right now? Sure. But looking at the long-term effects, they are not for me. I don't want to take medication so often that I need to take a liver function test to ensure that the medication is not causing further damage.

I think it's important to find an alternative to just simply taking medicine. Give it a shot. I mean, seriously. What harm can it do other than take up some time which is something we all have? Time.

SEEDS

☒ *Take music lessons on one or more instruments.*

☒ *Create your own out-in-public playlist or create your own lyrics*

☒ *Write your own song lyrics.*

3
THE GARDEN

The highest good is like water.
Lao Tsu

Who would have ever thought in a million years that I would want to be an organic farmer? Sure as heck not me. I was a professional landscaper for twenty years. I was pesticide-licensed in the state of Indiana for ten years. Additionally, I was part-owner for one of the larger, locally-owned companies in the city. When my father passed away in August of 2004, I decided I wasn't going to work in landscaping ever again. I was sick of it. What I want to do is own a farm, growing produce for local restaurants, stores, farmers' markets and churches. It's not quite the same as landscaping. However, there are a ton of similarities like dirt, seed, water, fertilizers and much more. I am about to get back into growing and planting things just as I did for twenty years, only this time without chemicals.

In 2011 I went to my therapist and was discussing everything that had happened over the previous few weeks: how I had screamed down a Soldier for no reason, how I had on a pretty regular basis yelled at my wife while having a conversation about her day. Things like this happened on a pretty regular basis. When I was done talking and listening to my therapist (as usual), I posed this question:

"Every few weeks I come and talk and talk and you listen. But it never feels like I accomplish anything other than talking. Aren't you supposed to recommend things for me to try in between visits?"

"Get a dog or start a garden or something" was her response. So that day I went home and said, "Baby, my therapist said I need to get a dog." That went over like a fart in church. My awesome and loving wife said "What else did she say?" So, instead, I started a garden. It started out with a four-foot-by-four-foot box made of one-inch-by-twelve-inch boards. I now have three boxes the same dimension, two twenty-five gallon buckets, four five-gallon buckets, and multiple planters and homemade pots. And it has been a ton of fun and not a whole lot of work. Don't get me wrong, I know that having a farm will be much harder than having a small garden. But it is so amazing to see how much I have learned and been able to accomplish in my small garden during the last two-and-a-half years. I plan on taking everything I have learned and utilizing it on a much larger scale.

The thing about all-organic gardening is two-fold. First, it is so much healthier for you than conventionally grown food with all its pesticides, hormones, and whatnot. Two, it forces me to spend time pulling weeds, watching for bugs, and much more. I honestly don't spend more than fifteen minutes a day in my garden. Over the last two-and-a-half years my family has saved over $2,000 in organic produce alone. I started off by jumping in with both feet. We went to our local organic store, bought seed, and started planting. Now, do you have to do it all organically? Not really. But it gives you more to do and it is so much healthier for you. You can even *taste* the difference.

I have a set routine now. I get off work, come home and go to my garden. I pull weeds daily which means only pulling a handful or a little more, checking under leaves for stink bug eggs, and looking for slug damage and other disease to my plants. When I'm done, I spray my plants with a pesticide-free mixture that detours bugs (water, Castle soap, and cayenne pepper is all it takes to detour the majority of damage-causing pests). No matter how crappy my day at work has been, I am relaxed, decompressed and ready to chill with my family by the time I am done in the garden. My wife can attest to how much it has helped.

I feel like this is one of the major reasons those of us with PTSD are always on guard or hyper-alert. We don't allow ourselves a chance to decompress. We need time. We need a small amount of time each day. PTSD makes you feel like your marriage is coming apart. You can't stop yelling at your spouse or kids. You are constantly in conflict at work. And most of it can be averted just by taking some peaceful alone time. Just spend fifteen or twenty minutes a day doing something that takes your mind off everything you just did at work. Do that, and when you walk back in the house you will actually feel refreshed. When you allow the stress to go away, you won't believe how much more relaxed you will feel, not just emotionally, but physically as well. You carry that mental stress in your muscles: your shoulders, neck, arms, back, and chest. Once we find an outlet, it will simply melt away. It's not an overnight sensation. It takes time, patience, and the understanding of those who love us.

If you are willing to try gardening, I can assure you that it is so easy to get started and it pays for itself. With a minimal investment you can make your money back and then some in your first year. If you are willing to get started, you can find a list set-up for building a raised bed at the end of this book. It also contains a list for containers for gardening with pictures of things you can use or, as I say, re-purpose. There are so many things you can use, even if you don't want to spend money. You can start with a bell pepper from the store, a one-gallon milk jug, and some dirt from your back yard. It really is that simple.

Try this: take an empty milk gallon jug and rinse it well. Cut the jug all the way around about three inches from the bottom. Flip the top over and set it inside the base. Take a coffee filter or a paper towel and line the neck so that when you add dirt it will not spill out. Place two inches of dirt and then an unbroken egg and fill it with dirt. Set it aside so the dirt will settle. Remove the seeds from a bell pepper (whichever color you prefer). Set them on either a paper towel or a plate to dry for three days. Plant two to three seeds in your jug ¼ of an inch in the dirt 2-3 inches apart from each other (you can plant more than one seed to improve your odds of one of them growing). At this point you fill the base with water and set in a warm area that has good lighting from a window or light. And there you have it: you just made a planter and planted peppers and it cost you nothing. You already had the gallon jug and the pepper. You got the dirt from your yard. And it took you five minutes of total work just to get started.

You now have a sense of accomplishment. You will have some peppers in a few months, and you get to watch your plant grow. The cool thing is you that only have to water it once to twice a week, because having the planter inverted and placed within the base creates a self-watering planter from scratch. Not only did it not cost you a thing, but as soon as you start harvesting peppers from it you will begin saving money. The possibilities are limitless.

As you take care of it and make more or get into a

raised bed, you will be taking your mind off of all the crap from your day. It gives you the chance to relax and then spend not just time, but quality time, with your spouse and family. In the end that is one of the main reasons to give this a try: so that our time with our families is quality time and not filled with tension and arguing.

I would get all worked up over nothing. If my son missed some dishes when cleaning up after dinner, I ended up yelling at him instead of simply telling him to finish cleaning. As I started raising my voice, I started an internal argument with myself. *Why are you yelling? Why are you raising your voice? There is no reason for this! You are still doing it!* And that made me angrier that the actual situation. But I wasn't able to back down anymore. The adrenaline would become too great. and I was in for the roller-coaster ride of emotion, followed by guilt (self-imposed of course).

But I fully believe that it was all because I never gave myself a chance to relax. I never let go of the day's events. After my deployment I had lost the ability to let things simmer down. I had a crazy need to win everything I was involved with, and I couldn't be wrong no matter what the situation.

Another reason I like using the garden is because when you first harvest a vegetable, you realize *I did this.* You develop some self-worth again. You feel like *Hey, I accomplished something. I'm not a waste.* It can actually make you feel as if you matter again. That is a huge part of dealing with PTSD. Of all of the things that we put ourselves and our friends and family through PTSD gives us a feeling of worthlessness. It can be so demoralizing.

Then in come the thoughts of suicide or thoughts of hurting others. Most of us with PTSD honestly don't want to hurt anyone. But the thoughts do occur.

We need to take active control over our thoughts, too. When we start directing the path that our thoughts take, this can help immensely. If you have headphones on with some of your favorite music playing all while weeding your garden and checking to see if there is any produce you can harvest for that night's dinner, do you even have time to think about how crappy your day was? I'm not talking about avoidance: I'm talking about control. Let's take active control of our thoughts. Stop allowing our minds to take control. They will screw us over almost every time. Given the chance to wander, your mind will immediately gravitate to what fills it the most (most what?). Sometimes it's that adrenaline-burnt memory section of combat or however you received your PTSD.

Wherever the mind goes, you will follow. When you allow your mind to lead you while it is relaxed and untrained, it will go where the strongest emotion is. The strongest is memory. For someone who suffers from PTSD, it's usually the significant life event that they experienced. It's a scar: an emotional scar that one has to try and take care of so it becomes as invisible as possible. Take control of your thoughts. Fill your time with an active process. The garden can give you just that. There a thousands of videos on Youtube that you can watch that will teach you almost everything you need to know about how to create, maintain, and use a home garden. And it doesn't matter if you live in an apartment or a house.

I can't stress enough that this is *not* avoidance. It is being active so that the intrusive memories do not take control. Instead of allowing the mind to lead us, we need to take charge and direct the path it is on. It's the same thing we do with our children or employees or subordinates: give them a path to be on and supervise them. Watch for the pitfalls and offer to give them guidance. Stop sitting back and waiting for the worst to happen. Believe me: that is a road you don't want to go down.

If you live in an apartment and don't think you have the room to garden because you don't have a yard, try this: use the same container I mentioned earlier. Last winter I grew basil, parsley, tomatoes, and sweet peppers in our upstairs bedroom. All it took was three pots, two of them being gallon jugs. Another thing you can do is take an old beach bucket and a shorter, wider bucket and make a self-watering pot by drilling a couple holes in the bottom of the beach bucket and placing it in the second bucket.

There is something to be said about growing your own food. It is calming and fulfilling. You take dirt, seed, water and time to watching the miracle of it all take place. For example, one little cabbage seed, which is only a millimeter in diameter, grows into a plant that is ten to twelve inches wide and two to three feet tall when completely mature. It is absolutely amazing to watch it happen. Another example is a single seed of okra (the size of a bead) grows to be seven to eight feet tall and has produced thirty to forty pieces of okra. That's all from one seed!

You get to watch as it goes from seed to sprout to flowering, giving off produce you can eat. Last night we went to Walmart and I (as usual) got lost in the lawn and garden center. We came across some sweet basil that was ready to be transplanted into the ground and was priced at $4. It was a non-organic variety and had almost no scent whatsoever. I have two basil plants right now growing that are around a foot tall, and you can smell them from about three feet away. You don't really notice these things until you have gardened on your own.

Using my garden as a form of self-therapy has been an amazing road-trip. I come home, kiss my wife and kids hello and head to the back yard. Nothing from work that day exists in my garden. It's just me, my plants and time working in the ground. Like I said, right now I have only three four-foot-by-four-foot beds to pull weeds. And not using herbicides and pesticides provides me with the take time to maintain it. Because I am not using pesticides for insect control, I have to visually inspect my plants. I take the time to see if there is any damage or if there are eggs anywhere. But it doesn't consume so much time that I no longer have time with my family.

I'm not saying this method will work for everyone, but isn't it at least worth a shot? I was so tired of being stressed and ready for an argument because of PTSD that I was willing to try anything. But I fully believe that it starts as an internal choice, a mental and emotional decision to make a change. I know that before I deployed to Iraq I was a different man than I am now. It got to a point where I was no longer happy with who I was, with how I was treating my wife and children or with the thoughts and nightmares I was having. Do you have to use a garden? No, you can use whatever you want. But don't avoid what you are going through. Avoidance will only cause the problem to compound. Take an active and aggressive role to make a difference in your own life as well as in the lives of the people you love.

One of my brothers and best friends with whom I deployed to Iraq has made some great strides in his own life to make a difference in others. He created STAGREPA, a way of life and a way to take active control over who he is and how he does things. STAGREPA stands for *Stand Aggressive, React Passive.* He modeled it after Jesus. Jesus stood firm in His beliefs but was passive in His outward appearance. Stand firm in what you believe. Have conviction in it. But don't lash out or be angry at the situation. Be passive and willing to self-search and grow. I would like to thank Jason for the mentoring he gave me in this area even if he didn't know that he had done so. Thank you, Jason. Strength and Honor!

This again boils down to making a choice not to be victimized by our situations and to take action by leading ourselves in positive ways. For me that is by being active in my garden and not allowing my daily crap and work-load to overwhelm me. I am challenging you: if you have PTSD or know someone who does, try this. Be understanding to the one who does, and lend a listening ear when they need it. Encourage them to pick up a hobby, no matter what it is: gardening, fishing, art, music, anything.

In the back of this book are pictures of some of the garden ideas you can use. If you have your own lawn or live in an apartment with limited space, you can still have a productive hobby with growing. You're not just growing food or plants. You are growing as a person! You will be taking an active step in your own recovery and therapy.

SEEDS

☒ *Plant something small and easy.*

☒ *Plant something you know you will eat or use.*

☒ *Season-permitting, plant directly into the ground, or into a container above or inside the ground.*

4
FAITH

The free man is a warrior.
F.J. Chu

If you are completely against Christianity or anything that has to do with God, then feel free to skip this chapter. Just understand that it has had a huge impact on my during my healing process. This chapter might get a little preachy, but, hey, my goal is to become a pastor.

I grew up in Fort Wayne, Indiana which is known as the city of churches. My mom took me to church off-and-on as a child, and I can't remember a summer where I didn't go to Vacation Bible School. I accepted Jesus as my Savior when I was 11-years old. And like most young people who were not fully immersed in the church, I fell away pretty quickly. I have always had a faith in God, but I didn't always practice my faith. I guess that can be said about many of us as we go through life. I am a Christian. Each of us who are have been called to be disciples and to spread the Word of God and God's love to the world.

I plan to go to school to become a pastor when I retire from the Army. After spending seventeen years in the Army and meeting thousands of people, I have met, worked with and become friends with people of multiple faith backgrounds: Muslim, Catholic, Jewish, Messianic, Baptist, Protestant, Lutheran, Satanic, Pagan, Wiccan and Atheist (I see being Atheist as being a system of faith. To me it takes a lot of faith to believe there is nothing to believe in).

I'm not going to tell you that you have to be a Christian to believe in God. You honestly don't. It's your choice as a human that the Creator has given you. Would I like for you to be a believer and accept the love God has for you? Without a doubt. But that is a part of one's free will. Even the Army (that does not support any one individual religion) still recommends that you have faith in something.

Every year we take several classes on Resiliency Training. It lists several pillars of life that help us to become more resilient and in order to be able to bounce back after a traumatic event. One of those pillars is faith. It is a fundamental truth that someone who has faith in a higher power is able to recover from a traumatic event quicker than one who doesn't have faith. If it wasn't for the fact that I have a strong faith that God loves me and wants what's best for me, I might have committed suicide (It is a thought that has crossed my mind frequently in the worst of moments).

I'm not saying that because I have faith in God nothing bad is ever going to happen in my life. If I thought that, I would be living a lie. Millions of people before me have had stronger faith than I do and have had horrible things happen to them. But knowing that there is a life after this, knowing that there is a place and time when I will no longer be suffering any physical, mental or emotional pain gives me hope. We have probably heard that the definition of having faith is to believe in something you cannot see. I disagree. I say we can see God in everything and everyone.

I talked earlier about the miracle of watching a plant grow from a small seed. Some almost two small to see yet they produce such huge things. Think about an apple tree. Look how small the seeds are in an apple the next time you eat one. Yet this large tree grows and produces more apples that each have within them the ability to reproduce more trees. It is a self-perpetuating cycle of life. Just like humans. An egg and a sperm come together and create human life. Those two things are so small they almost cannot be seen with the naked eye. Yet people grow to be upwards to six and seven feet tall.

You see the intelligent design of God's will in everything from a zucchini to an oak tree and from an amoeba to a human. We have been given an opportunity to create and maintain life, regardless of the fact that it is a piece of produce to eat or grass to maintain soil erosion. It doesn't take a lot of faith in anything to see that this didn't just happen.

A few years ago I was taking a college biology class and had to do a research paper on Darwin's theory of evolution. As I got into the study of it, you can actually see how insects, birds, fish and animals will adapt to where they live. I wouldn't call it *evolve.* They simply adapt. If you take a bird from the Amazon Rain Forest that has never been in North America and release it into a wild area, it will adapt. It will find food, and build a nest. The bird will do what it needs to in order to survive. Insects have been known to change their color patterns in one generation to adapt to their environment so that they can survive. It's God's plan in action: life begetting life. If we were to eradicate all of the flies on the planet, the amount of trash and number of animal carcasses left to decompose would be so much slower. There is a purpose for everything.

When I first met Robbie Grayson, we were talking about my experiences in Iraq as a Line Medic and as an Infantry Squad Leader. As a Christian and as a human, when you go to war, you are called to do things against the normal course of human nature. Shooting at or killing another person or seeing friends and brothers and sisters-in-arms getting shot or blown up right in front of you can be catastrophic. You cannot see all of that, go through it and say that you come home unchanged.

Robbie asked me what I attribute to my PTSD and why I haven't gone, for lack of a better word, crazy. I stand firm to this day that God allowed me to develop PTSD in order to be a help to others who have it. Honestly, if you have a problem with anything, to whom would you go? Someone who has never personally dealt with it or someone with a background in it? If I am having problems in my marriage, am I going to go to a counselor who has never been married? More than likely, no.

I'm not saying that going to school to get an education is not valid. I am saying that I would go to someone who has a personal connection with what I have experienced. Most of us are more than likely in that same category. The way I see it is like this: God allows things to happen or come into our lives for a specific reason. To build us up and make us stronger that we might be a better witness for spreading His Word and His love to others.

It's not a punishment. It's a development. If you didn't go through the things you have, you wouldn't be who you are today! That is a fact! I would prefer for all of you to have a relationship with God. By statistics I have already lost thirty percent of the people reading this. Not everyone will accept God's love or His sacrifice. Yes, He has made sacrifices for all of us. Let's look at John 3:16: "For God so loved the world that He gave His only begotten Son. That whosoever believeth in Him shall have everlasting life and not perish." The only genetic offspring that He will ever have, He allowed His Son to be born, separated from Him. Allowed Him to grow, develop and choose for Himself. And then allowed the people He created and chose to be His to berate, hate and reject Him. Finally, He watched as His Son was murdered and humiliated more than any man in history or in the future.

Is that not enough of a show of love? He allowed His Son who was love to become completely beaten and killed so that all of us, not just the chosen tribes of Israel, could have access to His kingdom.

My point is simply this: don't go through life thinking there is nothing out there. You can see the beauty of creation in everyday life. You can see it in music, art, social interaction, between animals and people and so much more. Step outside and look at the sky, how beautiful the colors are. Don't sit at home and wallow in self-pity and wonder *Why me?* Take action and control over your thoughts. Lead your mind, don't follow it. It will lie to you.

They say that there is no such thing as a recovered alcoholic, that no one ever fully recovers from an addiction. Bull. That is negating the healing power of God. It is putting a limit on His power and love for us. What has to happen is first to acknowledge that there is an addiction, a problem or something wrong in your life. Then you have to actively seek healing for it. There is nothing so hard or bad that God cannot overcome it. Believe that! If you are already a Christian, you know this. The problem is that we as believers in Him never fully let go of the flesh and allow the spirit to be our guide.

Yes, I am saying that there is such thing as a recovered alcoholic or drug addict, porn addict, sex addict or whatever other sort of addict. Stop limiting God and putting Him in a box like He is only able to do so much. God's power and love is limitless. Have full faith that you can and will be delivered from whatever is holding you back. You can have a full recovery. By saying that you can't, you are actually creating a self-defeated attitude. Nothing good comes from that. If you start something, believing that you cannot do it, you won't. David didn't go into battle with Goliath thinking he was going to lose. He went in saying he could do it. He went in saying "I will slay this giant who mocks my God."

Philippians 4:13 says "I can do all things through Christ who strengthens me". It doesn't say "some things" or "most things" it says all things. You can recover fully from any addiction. It doesn't mean you won't have some scars or some memories from it, but you can be fully healed. You can fully overcome whatever it is. You just have to have faith in God and take an active step forward. David didn't sit around and wait for God to get rid of Goliath. He stepped out in faith and took ownership of the situation. I am challenging you to do the same.

Step out in faith. Believe in your heart that God can and will heal you. But don't sit on your butt and wait. Nothing good comes to those who sit around instead of work. You have to be willing to put in the work. God doesn't reward the lazy, He rewards those who are willing to pull their weight and get things done. If you sit on your butt and do nothing to help in the process of healing, nothing is going to get any better. So get a move on it, pray and get on it.

I hear from so many people that they have to get "clean" before they can come to God, that He will never accept them because of what they have done in their past or with what they are struggling right now. But that is so not true. Paul, who was the first missionary to the Gentiles, was a murderer. He lived by the letter of the law. Only one man has ever lived a life that would honor the laws of the Old Testament: that is Jesus.

God doesn't call the sanctified and righteous. He sanctifies the called. We are so burdened by what we have done in our past. But here is the thing: we don't live there anymore. 2 Corinthians 5:17 says, "Therefore, if anyone is in Christ he is a new creation. The old has passed away; behold, the new has come." You are no longer tied to the way you were before. You are a new person, born again, and are not held accountable in Gods eyes. So the biggest obstacle is getting over ourselves. The *Lord's Prayer* is another great example of self-healing. It starts with forgiveness.

First, we have to be able to forgive ourselves. If we can't do that we will never be able to move forward. Matthew 6:14-15 says "For if you forgive others their trespasses, your Heavenly Father will also forgive you. But if you do not forgive others their trespasses, neither will your Father forgive your trespasses." I fully believe this extends to us as well. If you can't forgive yourself, then why would He forgive you?

As a Soldier we are called to do things that go against our beliefs as a Christian. But it doesn't mean we are going to Hell because we sinned. It means we need to forgive ourselves for having done what we were called to do as a Soldier. Once we do that, God will lift the burden of guilt from us.

It doesn't mean go out and be crazy and just forgive yourself. It means understand that you had no other choice and that it was wrong. But because we seek His forgiveness and then forgive ourselves at the same time, we are no longer held accountable for it or tied to it.

I believe that is why most of us continue to struggle with our PTSD more than we have to struggle. We aren't willing to forgive ourselves for the things we had to do in the heat of battle. Let's be frank here: war is Hell. There is nothing in the world that I can think of that compares to it. But we were the less than 1% of our nation who were called to be Soldiers. We volunteered to serve, knowing the chances that we might have to go to war.

SEEDS

- 🗷 *Get involved in a local faith community*

- 🗷 *Make it a habit to pray. Even if you find it awkward.*

- 🗷 Look around for like-minded people.

5
NUTRITION

Eating is even more important than the Emperor.
Chinese Proverb

Man has been in some state of war or conflict since the beginning of time, starting when Cain murdered Abel. But let's not go that far back at this time. Instead, let me start with my family's history with war. My grandfather fought in World War II and in the Korean War. My father was in Germany during the Berlin Crisis. Every male in my family has served in the military since the Revolutionary War. I seem to find myself asking *Why is it that we Soldiers today seem to be suffering from PTSD so much more than our fathers, grandfathers, and so on?*

In my opinion it has nothing to do with being more or less mentally fit than generations of the past. It has nothing to do with being more resilient. I think it can be traced to two things: nutrition and separation from what this nation was founded on as a nation that honors God. Let's talk about nutrition first. Faith involves my personal opinion based on my own research and I promised earlier that I wouldn't try to convert anyone.

How many minerals and vitamins are in the average piece of produce today? There aren't even half as many as there were in our ancestors' day including one generation ago. There has been a dramatic shift in commercial farming and the way food is produced and grown. Enter 1994 when Genetically Modified Organisms (GMO) were introduced into the food market for human consumption. Prior to this advent, GMOs were used to feed chickens, cows and pigs (not humans) in the 1980s. When we eat a steak, we ingest everything the cow has eaten. How is this possible? When we eat anything at all it is digested and absorbed into our body through the stomach and then the intestines. Then it is used to fuel the body's cells to keep us mobile and healthy. So when the animal is eating the GMO crop, it is being digested into the stomach and then through the intestines where it becomes fuel for the body's cells.

It's a proven fact that the average human can carry between 4 to 10 pounds of fecal matter in the colon and intestines. As it sits there, the body will still absorb waste which creates small amounts of toxemia.

When you eat chocolate, the chemical properties of it tell our bodies to release endorphins which are the chemicals in the body that make you feel good or euphoric.

Now, I am by no means a hippy. I love hunting, sports and action movies. I am, for all purposes, a man's man. But there is something to be said about the natural healing that can occur from our diet. Humans have been doing it for years. It has only been a short period of time since man has discovered parts of science where we can almost create our own types of medicine.

If all of this worked, why would there be a mass movement among people in America to go back to plant-based medicine and Eastern-style medicine which consists of changing your diet? Not only are conventional medicines starting to become addictive, but they may result in a host of other problems called "side effects." Why in the world do I want to take a medicine that could cause me to have a psychotic episode if I discontinue its use? That makes no sense to me. Try watching a television commercial for a new medication, and it has about 50 possible side effects. I think I will pass on that.

I have searched for some type of study on how nutrition helps with healing and regulates the chemicals in the brain. In essence how can I change my diet in a way that will affect healing from stress, depression, PTSD? Believe it or not, there isn't much out there. Almost nothing. I take PTSD medications for stress and anxiety, for sleep issues, and then there are the ones for my cholesterol, heartburn, chronic pain and more. I with my wife went to our local, health food store and started asking questions. I found that there are hundreds, if not thousands, of organic and/or herbal replacements for these medications.

I started taking Kava Kava root for my temper and anxiety. It is an organic root grown in the Tongan Islands. Its main principal is that it increases the brain's production of serotonin. Aren't Paxil, Celexa and Prozac considered serotonin-based medications? Why take a pill that is a chemical when I can take something that will cause my body to produce it naturally? Instead of taking Seroquel for my sleep and nightmare issues, I started taking Melatonin with 5htp. Seroquel is used to treat bi-polar disorder. It has a side effect of lowering your blood pressure in order to allow you to sleep orr to put you into a deep enough sleep that you don't dream. That's another chemical that the body doesn't produce and that has a list of side effects that are too long to count.

After we started our garden, my wife and I also decided to start eating healthier: more organic produce, hormone free meat and eggs. The major thing I've noticed is that I hardly ever get sick with a common cold. We spent weeks watching every documentary on Netflix you can think of about nutrition and diet. I'm not telling you to stop taking your medication. What I am telling you is that there are other options. Look into it. Just because it worked for me doesn't mean it will work for you. But who knows? It might. I don't know how many vets I have talked to who have jobs like driving rigs or working as security guards who, when taking a medication like Prozac, find it difficult to keep their certifications. There is a chance that the organic option could be even that much more beneficial.

Here's the thing: your body in all its systems is balanced. Wen everything works in harmony, we call it *homeostasis.* There is a vitamin or an herb or spice or seasoning that provides your body what it needs. Did you know that with depression there are tons of people who have increased their intake of Niacin to 500mg or more (of course this is a variety that is non-flushing) and have come out of their depression fully? It can be done. Listen to your body, go to your local health food store and grow organic produce of your own. Get healthy physically and it will greatly improve your mental health as well.

SEEDS

☒ *Pick a food you like. Find out how it gets to your plate.*

☒ *Watch a documentary on nutrition.*

☒ *Find a good multivitamin.*

6
THE HIDDEN HERO

You can never invite the wind,
but you must leave the window open.
Bruce Li

After I conducted interviews on Veterans and current members of the Army who are diagnosed with PTSD, I thought to myself *What about the spouses and loved ones? What are they doing behind the scenes that is helping their Veteran?* It's the spouse who is behind the scene supporting and loving their veteran. It is the family member who is doing so much even if all he or she does is listen to and love their veteran, an unsung hero. To them I say T*hank you for all you do and all you put up with.*

It has for a long time been my opinion that there is a critical component to the healing process. That essential piece is the spouse and/or loved ones of the Soldier with PTSD. I can attest to this personally: my wife like all spouses of Soldiers is amazing. She puts up with so much from her Combat Veteran. My wife and other spouses become the rock that we, the Soldiers, lean on. They are the ones upon whom we hope to rebuild the foundation of who we are.

Over the last few months I have been honored to get to know Melissa Seligman, founder of *Her War, Her Voice*. Her organization and my wife are the inspiration for this chapter. Melissa is also the spouse of a Soldier who has deployed and deals with PTSD. During our conversations we have both come to fully agree on this simple principle: I cannot help my spouse heal if I don't get myself back into balance as well. It, of course, goes both ways. When we are deployed, our spouses go through a huge array of emotional distress. This distress can be anything from missing the husband/wife, worrying if they will come home alive, being angry at them for being in the military or for subjecting them to this life. *Her War, Her Voice* is all about that part: healing the spouse.

Spouses play such a pivotal role in the recovery of their Veteran, and most of them don't even realize how important they are in the healing process. In order for them to be strong enough again to help their Veteran begin or improve on his/her journey of healing, they have to have the time to heal themselves first. Some of you might think this is selfish in its motive. It is not. I react to my wife's emotions just like she reacts to mine. So in order for me to heal and get better, so does she.

Most spouses have gone through multiple combat deployments. No one deployment is like another. My wife can tell you that. Even if they are sent to the same place doing the same job, most Soldiers will tell you that they are not at all similar. We Soldiers are so used to putting others first. We need to, specifically with our spouses, take care of them so they will be able to assist us once we begin our healing process. Then and only then will we be able to let go and start healing.

I know if it weren't for the love of my wife then I probably wouldn't have even cared and would have spiraled down further and further once I was diagnosed with PTSD. Our spouses don't suffer from their own cases of PTSD, but they suffer from the fallout of ours (the Soldiers). I'm not trying to make you feel like crap over the situation you are in. It's just a fact. The Bible says that the two come together and make one flesh. So if one part of our flesh is sick or hurt, it is going to affect the rest of it. I'm not the first to say it, but here it goes: Thank you so much for all you do as military spouses! We wouldn't be who we are if you weren't who you are in our lives!

I wonder if anyone is pondering the title of this chapter *The Hidden Hero.* The spouse gets hidden behind their Veteran regularly. We as Soldiers are constantly called *heros* in the news, in songs and by the people at the local restaurants who offer to buy us a meal. But with all that our spouses go through by simply supporting us, it is my opinion that they are just as heroic as we are (and I do not consider myself to be a hero by any stretch of the imagination). But maybe that's just me. It's ok. I've been wrong before, but I don't think I am this time. Just saying.

So this is my challenge to you as a Combat Veteran: even if you don't think your loved one has gone through half as much as you have, reconsider that train of thought. Support them. Your spouse needs you and needs to know that you still need them. One of the most common themes I have heard from the groups of military spouses I have interviewed has been the random change in emotions and stress each time their vet deploys. Here is just a short list:

- ☒ I miss them so much! Please come home soon and safe.

- ☒ I don't know how many times I can handle seeing you leave me for war.

- ☒ I am strong enough for us both. I will hold down the fort while you are gone.

- ☒ I am so proud of my vet! I support them 100%.

- ☒ Are you seriously leaving me again? I'm pregnant and how many anniversaries are you going to miss?

This is why I am so glad to have met Melissa and some of the ladies from *Her War, Her Voice.* Family Readiness Groups (FRGs) are great in concept but because of the human element involved can quickly deteriorate. I have personally seen them used as a social club to go out and party while their vets are gone. And I have seen spouses excluded because of their personal beliefs. It's not all of them; it is mostly only a select few. I feel that groups like HWHV have the potential to assist in the healing of the support channel of their vet.

We are only as strong as our weakest link. If a part of our chain (marriage) is hurting or scared or broken, we need to do everything in our power to help them just like they do for us. I love my wife, Paige, with every part of my being, and I can honestly say I am so sick of having a short temper that it angers me. It can at times create a vicious, masochistic cycle, a roller-coaster cycle which I am sick and tired of. My wife deserves better than that from me.

So I am begging you, as a husband who wants only the best for his wife or as a wife who wants only the best for her husband, to help her/him find someone to reach out to: groups like HWHV who play a pivotal role in healing and finding support the way that you need.

I want to encourage you, the military spouse or loved one of a Veteran, to do more than just sit at home and assume that you can't handle it. It's not just about you just as Soldiers know it's not just about us. Seek out the help you need. Find a group like *Her War, Her Voice*. Go to counseling on post or through *Military One Source*. And for the love of Pete, don't wait. Do it *now*. A lot of our frustrations come from seeing how it is affecting you. When my wife is in a bad mood or her depression is kicking in or whatever. it affects me as well. I am very empathetic of her feelings, and I hate seeing her go through these difficult times.

Now, to the Soldiers: tell your spouse how much you appreciate all that they are doing for you. Let them know how you much it means to you. If you see them struggling with their emotions, offer to help them set up an appointment or find someone to talk with. Help them first so they will be able to once again pick up the slack when you go get the help you need to deal with your own issues. Be their rock and their place of comfort. This is honestly one of the hardest areas for me. My wife tells me how frustrating it is that she can't be mad. She gets angry, and I get angry because I don't like seeing her that way. I'm not even mad at her. I just don't want her being stressed out. It's a work in process, but it takes both of us willing to work on it in order to succeed.

SEEDS

☒ *Tell your hero that you love them.*

☒ *Thank your hero for their patience and understanding.*

☒ *Help your hero find a support group that will help them to be better equipped to support you.*

46

7
OUR OWN WORST ENEMIES

*I have humility enough to confess my errors
and to retrace my steps.*
Confucius

How many people are diagnosed with or suffer from PTSD today? Way too many or not enough? There are unfortunately those who have scammed the system and cheated their way into a diagnosis simply so that they can reap the benefits. Then there are those who refuse to be treated because they don't want to be labeled. It doesn't help when you look in the news and see the crap that is going on in legislation. As we speak, there are bills in Congress that want to label all people diagnosed with PTSD as a threat or a risk. On August 31, 2012, President Obama Signed an Executive Order called *Executive Order -- Improving Access to Mental Health*

Services for Veterans, Service Members, and Military Families. I challenge you to google it and read the entire thing. You will see how it can be seen as something that is not positive for veterans.

Don't get me wrong. Some of us suffer so severely that we are a risk, but that number is so small compared to the number of us who aren't. As a nation we have created a stigma. *He/she is a veteran. He/she has PTSD, so he/she must be crazy and want to kill everyone around them.* Not true at all. For the majority of us, we simply don't like large crowds and would rather stay at home away from it all. We have become introverts. Because of all the media hype, we feel everyone else would be better off if we just locked ourselves up.

It's not really fair if you ask me. We owe more to our veterans than that. We can't allow this to keep happening. Reach out to someone you know and offer, at the very least, friendship. We are humans, after all, and we naturally crave companionship with one another. When you isolate yourself from the world you create a self-perpetuating cycle of ideas like *I don't deserve to be around people. I don't deserve to be normal.* Then the self-hate comes, often leading to suicidal ideations.

We put more pressure on ourselves than anyone else could even think about doing. I honestly believe it's one of the reasons we close ourselves away. When you are beating yourself up on a daily basis, when do you stop? When do you say "Stop. I've had enough"? You turn into a bully. *But your prey is yourself.*

We have become our own worst enemy. But there is also another spot where we become an even bigger enemy to ourselves. And that is thinking that because we served or deployed to combat that we are entitled to everything. Entitlement is something you earn, and, yes, we have earned some. Over the last few years I have seen so many warriors turn almost narcissistic when dealing with civilians. It grates the heck out of me.

Here is where I stand, and I have said it a few times already: "You will not heal without actively doing something to cause healing." We are told as warriors, "You're my hero" and so many things like that. But if you look in the mirror and you say to yourself *I am a hero,* then I have three words for you: GET OVER YOURSELF. We as a community don't join to become worshiped or seen as a hero. If you do, you came to the wrong place. We join to serve, to provide for our families or to be a part of something bigger than ourselves.

Every day 22-23 Veterans commit suicide. This does not include the number of attempts per day. Every 36 hours, one person on active duty commits suicide. This again does not count the number of attempts. This is a cry for help from our community of warriors.

The homeless rate for Veterans is higher than any other profession percentage-wise. Something has to be done, and it starts with caring and reaching out. Being a battle buddy doesn't end during peace-time or when you are not deployed.

You don't feel like you have a serious enough mission when you aren't in combat? Then start seeking out ways to help your fellow warriors here by showing them that you still care just as much as you did downrange.

SEEDS

- ☒ *When you are experiencing a difficult moment, do a simple, selfless deed.*

- ☒ *Remember that as a Warrior, it's your job to put others first*

- ☒ *Imagine how hurt others feel by seeing us hurt.*

8
TRAITMARKER & MORE

Talk doesn't cook rice.
Chinese Proverb

What defines you? No, really, what defines you? What makes up who you are? Have you ever taken a personality assessment? I never even thought about it until I met Robbie Grayson. Robbie reached out to me from a mutual friend. He is a big part of the reason I even decided to write this book and how I ended up co-authoring *TraitMarker-for Combat-related PTSD* (www.traitMarker.com). I have learned a ton about who I am and what makes me tick. I never honestly gave it much thought in the past. So when Robbie asked me to take *TraitMarker* I was a little skeptical.

When I took the assessment I found out three major things about myself: *Who I am, Who I am not,* and *Who I am becoming.   Who I Am:* I am an *Ender (Direction, Operation, Judgment).* For me it doesn't matter how things get accomplished so long as they do, and the process doesn't concern me as much as the desired outcome. *Everything* has to be finished. Of course, don't tell my wife that or she will call bull.

Who I Am Not: I am not a *Dreamer (Impression, Vision, Image).* What that means is that while I have Dreamer traits, they are not as positively passionate as my Ender traits. I am very artistic and focused on the journey. This is the supportive part of me. It's what everyone who comes to me sees me to be: the creative one who puts a lot of thought into what he is doing.

I'm naturally conflicted with myself between my Ender and my Dreamer. Take this and add PTSD to the mix and I'm ticked off at myself on a regular basis. I'm never happy with anything I'm doing or have done.

Who I Am Becoming: the third part of me is that I am becoming a *Guardian (Boundary, Rule, Policy).* Anybody who knows me knows that I can't stand bullies and that I will without hesitation defend someone who I feel is being bullied, put down or taken advantage of. I don't care if I know you or have never seen you before in my life. If you are acting like a jerk, I will confront you. Sometimes, that's not such a good thing, and sometimes it is. It all depends on the situation and what's going on around you, I guess.

So the three DNA strands of my TRAITMARK are *Ender, Dreamer* and *Guardian.* Once I realized what these meant, I was able to start paying attention to what I was doing in any given situation. I don't know how many times my wife has asked me to clean off my portion of the corner desk that we share. I just start throwing things away. It's the *Ender* in me. Then she goes through the trash and I'm in deep trouble because I've just thrown away pictures that the kids have colored and letters that they have written us and coupons and receipts that she wanted to keep. But I was *getting it done* in my head. I was being the *Ender.* What she came to me for was to be the *Dreamer.* I begin to put some thought into what I was doing and took time and effort to consider the process that I was implementing.

This is, of course, only one example. But I can honestly tell you that I have made a large amount of progress in dealing with my PTSD due to understanding *Who I am* with my personal TRAITMARK. So I encourage you to go to www.traitmarker.com and take it.

EMDR or *Eye Movement Desensitization and Reprocessing* is basically having you talk about the one most vivid memory or disturbing flashback all while following the movement of a finger or wand with only your eyes. It allows your brain to finally process information that was fragmented because the brain wasn't able to process it during the time of stress or chaos. I don't fully understand the science behind it, but from all the research I have done it seems to show major progress for those of us dealing with PTSD. I know that if I find a medical provider who offers it, I will be trying it.

That's for sure. I talked with Melissa Seligman from *Her War, Her Voice,* and she told me that her husband had amazing results from it. I honestly haven't heard anything negative about it.

It makes me wonder that if it is so awesome (and I'm not being sarcastic), why aren't the VA and the Military using this as a default when treating for PTSD? Every provider should be trained in it, so it *could* be done.

Here is what I would love to see happen: I would love to see every Warrior take *TraitMarker for Combat-Related PTSD* (www.traitMarker.com or contact Robbie Grayson at traitmarker.com and he will give you a free token to take it) before they ever deploy to a combat zone. Once they return, they can take their assessment profile to their provider which lets the provider know how the Warrior's brain is wired or how they tick. The provider gets a very accurate assessment of who you were *before* you deployed to combat. And by using that information. combined with EMDR and nutrition, it specifically targets you for your therapy session. I honestly believe it would be that easy!

A friend of mine reached out to me a while back and asked if I had ever considered getting a therapeutic massage to help with my anxiety. And, of course, until right then I hadn't. So I figured I would try anything legal at this point. So I went to *Studio K Massage* here in my local area. Kathy, the owner was amazing. Deep tissue, cupping, and healing touch were done over a period of 5 weeks, twice a week, and each of the methods each time. The emotional release from the healing touch (Chakrah alignment) was something that I had never before experienced. I seriously need to thank Kathy and her staff for offering the sessions to me.

These are all things I have tried:

- Music
- Worship
- Gardening
- Teaching gardening
- Massage therapy
- Writing songs
- Diet
- Organic Medication Replacement
- Baking bread
- Fishing
- Therapy
- Medication

So I've tried a lot. But maybe none of this looks appealing to you. The point is to *go out and find what works for you.* Be active, and do something about it. Don't just sit around and wait to get better.

SEEDS

- *Learn more about yourself.*

- *Remember who you were before you developed PTSD.*

☒ *Don't just sit and wait for things to happen. Make things happen.*

9
THE TRANSITION

Benefit comes from what is there.
Usefulness from what is not there.
Lao Tsu

I'm adding this Chapter in after 10 months of retirement. I honestly cannot believe that it has been this long since I got out. In January of 2014 I came to Franklin Tennessee to finally meet in person my publisher, Robbie Grayson, and his amazing family. We began looking for a house while we visited him for four days. We looked at three houses, and we got the last one we looked at in Brentwood, TN. *I'm loving life more than I ever have.*

19 of us Combat Veterans took a trip to California to meet with Dr. Genie Z. Laborde (influence-integrity.com) under the direction of Kathy Dent and Robbie Grayson.

We Veterans ranged from the combat zones of Vietnam, Somalia, Desert Storm, Iraq and Afghanistan. We were blessed with the opportunity to learn neuro-linguistic programming techniques (NLP) to aid in transition from one of the pioneers in that industry. It was pretty awesome: not going to lie. I've had the blessing of getting to know some of the best group of veterans ever. Radio hosts, fellow authors, musicians, and so much more.

I was also given the chance to sing in front of billionaires, the children of kings and queens from Africa and Asia, as well as people in the movie, television and music industry. It was pretty amazing! Not long after that trip, I was afforded the chance to be at the *Farmer Veteran Coalition* (FVC) national stakeholders' conference in Des Moines, Iowa . I made some amazing contacts.

There have been some hiccups along the way. But the one thing that I have going for me that other Veterans don't? A Mentor. Now, here's the best part (there *is* a method to my madness). In the Army we have what are called *battle buddies.* Whatever you do, wherever you go, you always have a battle buddy: someone who you trust and in whom you have confidence. Veterans by nature (specifically Combat Veterans) can be a very non-trusting people. I'm one of them. Luckily for me, I was able to get to know my Mentor over a two-year period before I needed to completely lean on him. Here is what I learned that I needed in my period of transition (This list covers before, during and after):

1. **A Mentor on the Outside**. Someone who has already transitioned or someone who is already in the area you are going, if it's somewhere new. Civilian "battle buddies" can work as well. They should be tied into the local networks of business owners or at least Veteran-friendly companies.

2. **A Solid Resume**. I cannot express enough how important this is. Most of us don't realize that our military occupations actually *do* transfer over to civilian skills. The key is in how we sell it. Here are two examples that a lot of us don't think about: equipment and accountability. I signed for 2.4 million dollars in Medical equipment while in Iraq. I owned it and took care of it and turned it in with *every penny accounted for.* So that responsibility translates into *accountability and supply resource management.* Let's be perfectly honest here. If you were in a leadership position of any kind, then you more than likely can use this kind of experience-situation in your resume. So it's helpful to have someone who can help you word your resume so that your military experience translates into a language that civilians will understand.

3. **Getting Plugged in**. If you're not going back to the place where you entered the military or before you entered, then you need to get plugged in. If you're going back home, then you need to get plugged back in! I can't express how important this is. My buddy and publisher, Robbie, lived for 16 years in the area where we decided to move. He is an entrepreneur and very tied in to the local area. He introduced me and my family to an entire network of people. By the time we ended up moving to Tennessee I had an entire network of friends and an interview for work already set up before I even walked into town. By having a Mentor, creating a solid resume, and getting plugged in I ended up walking into a house, job, and community of friends. It was seamless.

4. **Getting Tied in**. If you move to a completely new area like I did, then you need to get tied in to the local veteran community. I'm not talking about hanging out at the VA, VFW or DAV daily. What I am saying is to find some local vets. Connect and watch each others' backs. It will make you feel better to have someone with the same background. I was blessed enough not only to make great civilian friends, but I ended up getting tied into the local veteran community

and making some amazing connections as well. A good friend I made always says that we as Warfighters/Veterans need to have a mission. Not having a mission is one part of what is killing us. As a community, we are sitting on our butts and doing nothing. We are simply working our 9-5 or collecting our disability. Find a mission. Help others transition. Help others find a path to healing. Do something! Don't just sit there and wait for things to happen. Make them happen.

5. **Stay Off the Couch**. It all starts with a decision, not a choice. A choice is static: it has no intent or action to it. A decision has to be made by the Warfighter who needs healing. A decision is dynamic. The decision in itself is action. We not only need to take personal responsibility but personal action. We need to have the attitude of *Get off the couch and do something* in order heal. Pills and therapy are not a cure! They are tools. We need to open up and dig into our tool boxes and take inventory of the tools at our disposal. Warfighters at times don't give themselves enough credit when it comes to personal healing. Will this road-map work for all of us? NO. Just like PTSD doesn't affect each of us the same way. What does it boil down to? The decisions that we make. The problem, as I see it, is that we have blinders on to the options

laid out in front of us. It's a combat-created tunnel vision. Once we take off the blinders, we are able to see a wider range of options.

Gardening, fishing, models, art, music, helping other Warfighters, working out, sports, writing, learning something new: these are just the tip of the iceberg for options to a path of healing. But we can't do any of this by being passive about it. We can't just simply have a choice to make. We have to make a decision. Find a hobby you can get lost in: one that at the end of the day allows you to lose all track of time (This is where my TraitMarker *Guardian* comes into play). It's not avoidance, it's a distraction.... and a solution. It's a decision to get off the couch and take an active, aggressive stance in your personal healing.

When I talk about my situation, I call it *My PTSD.* I have taken ownership of it. I have made the decision to go after it rather than let it have ownership of me, allowing me to creating an area of active healing over passive healing. What has helped me has been three main pillars with a host of smaller ones. My three main pillars are my faith, my music, and my gardening: things for which I already had a passion. For others it might be something else. Whatever it is, you have to get up and start somewhere.

Why has gardening worked for me? First, it is that my hands are in the soil, allowing my skin to absorb the minerals. Second, it is seeing and assisting in the creation of life as opposed to seeing or inflicting death in war. It creates a balance that I have been missing. Hopefully, it will allow me to continue creating new memories that eventually override and replace the negative ones.

Music is a place where I probably will leave some people behind due to my feelings about it. Music and my faith are intertwined, and I speak only for myself on this part. When I got home from my first deployment, I scrubbed my entire music library and removed anything that wasn't from a "Christian" artist. I have since selectively added "Secular" musicians back in. Writing lyrics inspired by my internal struggles has allowed me the removal of all the negativity I had formerly experienced when returning home from combat. I needed upbeat and positive things coming in.

I also dug deeper into my Bible and focused more on my faith. For you, it might be something else. But let's be real: you have to start somewhere. I hope this helps you and that you share it with someone who needs help.

Now, understand that transition isn't just transitioning from the Military into the Veteran community. I also transitioned from medication to organic supplements. I'm going to give a list of the different things I take. I am not a medical doctor and am only telling you what I have used that has worked for me:

- ☒ *Anxiety and Depression:* Kava Kava powder. Kava is a root that grows in the Tongan Islands.

When taken, it creates a reaction in the intestines that causes your body to produce its own serotonin (the hormone in the body that helps with anxiety). Gaba is a natural mood elevator. I take 750mg a day. It helps with the dopamine receptors and with the ability not to hold onto anger when it arises due to a PTSD episode. I also use Niacin 500mg non-flushing. There are hundreds of studies of people who take high doses of Niacin to help with depression and have seen some phenomenal results. I'm one of them. I started taking these three supplements in place of a high dose of Celexa. Yes, it's three pills in place of one, but I no longer walk around smelling like a fecal factory. *True Story.* For added benefit I also take a B-12 and a B-complex.

☒ **Liver Support:** Due to the fact that Kava can cause damage to the liver if used for extended periods of time, I take a Milk Thistle supplement to help with cleaning and supporting my liver. Once a year, I go in and have what's called a Liver Function Test (LFT). So far, perfect levels!

☒ **Sleep:** I was on 50mg of Seroquel which totally burned my ability to fall asleep without it. Even doing a double shot of Nyquil wouldn't help because of how strong Seroquel is. And guess what one side effect is: suicidal ideation and fecal odor. Seriously! I can't make this up, people! After I transitioned from the Celexa to the alternatives I took about a week and then decided to start the transition from Seroquel to Melatonin with 5HTP. I actually went about 3 weeks with no sleep meds before I started taking the Melatonin 5HTP. The 5HTP is a heavy protein that helps the Melatonin get you into a deeper sleep once it kicks in. The great part is not feeling like a zombie in the morning!

- ☒ *Night Sweats:* Potassium, Magnesium, and D3. Studies have shown that the body, when night-sweating, burns excess amounts of Potassium and Magnesium. The problem is that the body won't absorb most of it without taking a D3 supplement. That's not really a big problem in my estimation. This helps one not to feel zombiefied in the morning. Again, I'm not a Doctor and I am not giving medical advice. This is a document of what I have done and what has worked for me. I have had hundreds of Warfighters come to me to ask what I am taking. I even had a Doctor at the VA give me kudos for what I am taking. I can tell you that since I have transitioned from the dope to the organics, I have felt better. If you want to try it, then I highly suggest doing it under a doctor's supervision. Good luck and God bless!

10
CLOSING THOUGHTS

*Never impose on others
what you would not choose for yourself.*
Confucius

I started writing this book as a way to share how I use specific things in my life to cope with my PTSD. I call it *My PTSD* simply because I have taken ownership of it. When you own something, you are in control of it. You make it work for you, or do what you want it to do. I'm not saying that I am in complete control of my PTSD. What I am saying, however, is that I am taking an active approach not to allow it to control me. So if you suffer from PTSD, I encourage you to do likewise. Stop fighting it and saying, *Not me. I'm not weak* or *This can't happen to me.* Own it. *I have PTSD, and I am going to do the best I can to control my own destiny.*

Those of us with PTSD have trigger: things or occurrences that set us off. For me it can be a few things such as loud noises, movies that make me relive past events, crowds in a store and so on. Pay attention to the moments when you get angry or become hyper-vigilant and see what is happening during those moments. Ask your loved ones to watch you and let you know calmly and gently when you are "in a moment." There are times when we are so caught up in the moments of our lives that it is hard to see what is actually going on. Sometimes, it takes a second set of eyes to see what we are going through in order to properly see what is happening to us. It honestly helps to have an objective opinion from the people we trust and love.

As I started writing, I wasn't really sure how I was going to tie all of the components together or how I was even going to get started. Writing this book has turned into another form of self-therapy. So for that, I want to say thank you to Robbie for giving me the idea. You rock, brother! It feels really good to get it out. I just love teaching and helping others.

Speaking of tying things together, did you know that music ties into your faith? It's a huge part of worship. David worshiped by writing songs and playing his harp. He showed praise to God by dancing and giving all glory to God. So I believe it is almost imperative that we as followers, as believers in God, worship Him with all we have. Music included. This for me is why I did the music scrub of my library.

I guess the biggest thing I hope people get from this is not to be afraid to seek help.

And for those who have loved ones who suffer with PTSD: be patient, be understanding, and show them love and support. Be there as a shoulder to cry on and know that they aren't mad at you. They simply do not understand what is going on with them, what they are going through or why. Let's try to break the stigma. Not everyone with PTSD is dangerous. Heck, the vast majority of us aren't. We don't want to hurt anyone. We just want to be treated the same as any other human being, and we want our loved ones to know that we are trying the best way we know to get better.

There is no one sure-fire way to treat PTSD, because it affects everyone a little differently. Soldiers are trained to be flexible, but at times it can feel so overwhelming that you want to break down. Sometimes while I am driving down the road, I have thoughts that seem tempting. You know:*If I just jerk the wheel into that pole or tree, I can call it a day and not have to worry about it or suffer anymore.* I try to shake those thoughts as soon as they emerge.

Don't isolate yourself. Find someone to whom you can talk. Find a friend, family member, priest, pastor, or minister... someone who won't make you feel judged. That in my opinion is the biggest problem with most of us: not seeking help. We are afraid that we are going to be judged, called weak, or dismissed as a crybaby. It's not weak to ask for help. On the contrary I think it's weak if you *don't* seek help. One of the pitfalls of dealing with PTSD is that you want to just crawl into a hole and hide from the world. Unfortunately, it's our family and loved ones who pay the biggest price for that.

For all of you out there who love someone with PTSD, thank you from the bottom of my heart for being there for them and for loving them. They need you now more than they will probably ever be able to tell you. Don't give up on them. Love them even if it means from a distance or allowing them to vent their frustrations. Just like recovering from an addiction, you have to admit that you have a problem in order to start the healing process. If you are not willing to accept that you have it, then you can never identify the problem and all you will do is mask it or cover it up.

Many turn to alcohol, drugs, promiscuity and other things to cope with PTSD. There is such a drastic change in who you've become that you end up taking drastic measures to become the "old" you again. As we all know, that can make things even worse. Now, you don't only have PTSD but you have an alcohol or drug addiction or an unwanted pregnancy or an STD. That just compounds the problem and creates a feeling of overwhelming burden, leading to either depression, more anxiety... or worse, suicidal ideations. Believe me, I have lost enough friends to suicide that I can promise you that it's not worth it.

I know that I have said it a few times that there is no one specific way to treat PTSD. The reason that I keep saying it is because of how true that statement is. There are so many factors to be considered: how we were raised, where we grew up, our overall personality and many other things. There is no one way to treat it. For some people just going to therapy sessions with a medical provider may be enough. There are others who need more than just therapy. From the literature I have studied lately, the Army has been trying new things like immersion therapy. Immersion therapy is simply exposing you to sounds, smells and visual stimuli in order to desensitize you to the things that are overwhelming you in your thoughts, memories and dreams.

Again, it is my opinion that you need to deal with it head on. Take ownership of it, and come out of denial. You were diagnosed with PTSD, so do something about it. Don't just sit on your butt and suffer in silence. Take an active role in your recovery. There are so many things that you can try or do in order to help yourself heal: therapy, hobbies, or talking to a friend who has been through the same things. If you sit and bottle it up, you will allow it to take over and have full control of what you do and how you react. It will consume you from the inside out. You owe it to yourself to be proactive. You are not helpless or weak.

The Combat Veteran has survived through so much turmoil and life-threatening situations, so don't allow PTSD to be your downfall. We are stronger because we have suffered and stronger because of what we have gone through. I constantly hear from people about how they wish they could go back in time and make changes or do something different. I say *Don't wish for that.* If you didn't go through those ordeals, you wouldn't be who you are today and eventually who you will become. We are on a constant journey in life. We are going to change one way or the other.

You didn't quit in combat when the going got tough, so don't quit on yourself now when you need it most. If there is any way you can treat yourself without the use of harsh medications, then I recommend that you do it. But remember that I am not a doctor and that all I can do is share my experiences and what I have learned on my own journey.

What have animals done for thousands of years when they have gotten sick? They go out in search for the scents of things that they know will make them better. There is an herb, leaf, root or plant that will pretty much cure whatever is wrong with us. Healthy, natural and nutritious foods have tons of healing properties. So why should we rely on big pharmacopeia?

I'm not saying to go and graze on the back forty and ignore your doctors. What I am saying is to start looking into drug-free alternatives. Take the time, do some research and talk to your doctor about it. If they won't discuss it with you, then go find a nutritionist. Nutritionists are well-respected and under-exposed professionals.

I believe that someone once said "Let food be thy

medicine." If you're sick, take some vitamin C or some Zinc. Are you depressed or overly-anxious? Try taking some Niacin and or a B-12. All of this can be found in natural food sources. A nutritionist knows these things. They can lead you to the proper food sources. I have spent a lot of time lately watching food documentaries and learning what's going on with our diet here in America. Why are we obese yet malnourished? Okay, sorry, I'm off my soapbox now. But look into it. It will change your mind about how you eat.

SEEDS

I may not have discussed something that interests you. What I talked about in the book is what I have done for myself. I challenge you to step out of your box and find something that you enjoy. Find something that will cause a natural distraction and allow you to relax. DON'T AVOID! Find at a minimum two hobbies: one for just you and one that is a joint hobby that you can do with your loved ones. Make it something that you will both enjoy.

11
GARDEN DESIGNS

The best fertilizer is the gardener's shadow.
Chinese Proverb

   Backyard gardens are so easy to get started. We
started our small garden for less than $300. It's a raised
bed system with three beds and six containers. There
are several different ways to set up a raised bed (and
you can customize it any way that you want). Here are
three different kinds we have set up. Listed below are
the dimensions and materials you will need to set it up.
All you have to do is till the ground and plant. It won't
cost you as much that way.

TYPE 1
[4 x 4 FOOT BED]

a. 1 x 12 four foot-long (4 boards)

b. 4-inch corner brackets (8 brackets. These usually come in packages of 4 with all the screws you will need).

c. Organic soil for growing vegetables (9 bags)

d. Various seeds for planting

TYPE 2
[2 x 8 FOOT BED]

a. 1 x 12 two foot-long 2

b. 1 x 12 eight foot-long 2

c. 4 inch corner brackets (8 brackets)

d. soil for growing vegetables (9 bags)

e. Various seeds for planting

TYPE 3
[3 x 8 FOOT BED]

a. 1 x 12 three foot-long 2

b. 1 x 12 eight foot-long 2

c. 4 inch corner brackets 8 total brackets

d. Organic soil for growing vegetables (9 bags)

e. Various seeds for planting

After you place the soil in your bed, allow it to settle for a minimum of two days for the air pockets to break down. This will help your seeds to germinate. One of the main keys to successful gardening is having as much seed-to soil-contact as you can get.

(On the following 2 pages page are examples of 2 simple garden beds I've made and 2 pictures of the results that I got from my garden)

12
LYRICS INSPIRED BY WAR

Those who hear not the music think the dancers mad.
Chinese Proverb

GRIND

(Written by Josh Head & Malachias Gaskin)

Do you see me rolling down
This road I'm walking
My eyes are stuck on the ground
People talking
Broken lives follow me around
But they can't break me
They can't see what I have found
And why it lifts me

As I grind on through this life
Can you take me
It will cut you like a knife
Will you take me
You can't hide light in the dark
It will always shine through
It will cut the ties that bind
And let you grind through

Darkness comes from all around
Closing on me
I won't let it put me down

I will push free
Scream out loud but make no sound
Please, hear my cry
Pull me up from the ground
Let the dark die

As I grind on through this life
Can you take me
It will cut you like a knife
Will you take me
You can't hide light in the dark
It will always shine through
It will cut the ties that bind
And let you grind through

Brighter days are coming round
I can feel it

No longer stuck in the crowd
And I won't quit
Broke the chains that kept me bound
And I am free now
Freedom from the dark is what I found
You broke it for me

As I grind on through this life
Can you take me
It will cut you like a knife
Will you take me
You can't hide light in the dark
It will always shine through
It will cut the ties that bind
And let you grind through

FREEDOM

(Josh Head, Eisner Gaitan, Sean Peabody & Gaskin)

Soldiers marching off to war
They don't question what they do it for
A greater cause than who we are
When we get there hit the floor

Close your eyes
See their face
If you can do it
Then take my place
Your heart will pound

Your pulse will race
And if you're still here
You can take my place

Brothers don't always have the same last name
This is why we will win this game
We're in control till the very end
Because our will, will not bend

Close your eyes
See their face
If you can do it
Then take my place
Your heart will pound
Your pulse will race
And if you're still here
You can take my place

Close your eyes
See their face
If you can do it
Then take my place

Your heart will pound
Your pulse will race
And if you're still here
You can take my place

YOU CAN'T TAKE MY
YOU CAN'T BREAK MY

YOU CAN'T HAVE MY
FREEDOM

YOU CAN'T TAKE MY
YOU CAN'T BREAK MY
YOU CAN'T HAVE MY
FREEDOM

PHOTOS

MY FIRST (1ˢᵗ) DEPLOYMENT

This was me before PTSD

Detonating a truck used as an IED (blurred)

Checkpoint 92

Weapons found during a raid

Grenades & Russian ammo

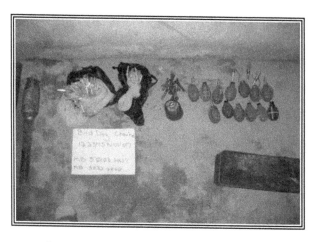

Grenades, detonation fuses, and an RPG

RPG's and Russian ammo

Deep freezer filled with ammo

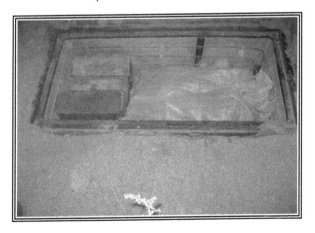

Another deep freezer

Preparing for an EOD mission at night

The morning after a firefight at Checkpoint 92

Damage from a .50 cal Russian to an armored window

PHOTOS

MY SECOND (2nd) DEPLOYMENT

As an Army bandsman

Playing music for the troops at COB Speicher

Opening for Vertical Horizon

RESOURCES

(Below are some of the resources I've used to participate in my active healing and to write the book)

Documentaries I watched about organics, the food industry, and nutrition:

Hungry For Change Directed by James Colquhoun, Laurentine Ten Bosch

Fat Sick and Nearly Dead Directed by Joe Cross, Kurt Engfehr

Forks Over Knives Directed by Lee Fulkerson

Vegucated Directed by Marisa Miller Wolfson

Food Matters Directed by James Colquhoun, Carlo Ledesma

Farmagedden Directed by Kristin Canty

Food Fight Directed by Christopher Taylor

Frankensteer Directed by Marrin Canell, Ted Remerowski

The Gerson Miracle Directed by Steve Kroschel

The World According to Monsanto Directed by Marie-Monique Robin

Genetic Roulette Directed by Jeffrey M. Smith

People I've interviewed

SFC Damon McCullough, United States Army, Combat veteran

SSG Iaian Thompson, United States Army, Combat Veteran

SGT Juan Palacios, United States Army, Combat Veteran

CPT Mike Mullaly, United States Army, Combat Veteran/Nurse

Melissa Seligman, Founder of "Her War, Her Voice"

Kristina Waters, "Her War, Her Voice"

Suzanne Baroody, Military Family Life Consultant

Robbie Grayson, Founder "TraitMarker" and "Traitmarker for Combat-Related PTSD"

Kathtin May, Owner "Studio K"

Gardening resources I've used

www.Growingyourgreens.com John Kohler

http://www.farmvetco.org The Farmer Veteran Coalition

Music resources I've used

http://www.singingsuccess.com/Singing

http://www.guitarcenter.com/ (Find a local or chain music store, and anyone working there can help you find someone to give you lessons).

Organizations for veterans web/facebook pages

http://www.facebook.com/TippingPointWithBooneCutler?hc_location=stream

Boone Cutler, Veterans Rights Advocate/Radio Host/Combat veteran

http://www.facebook.com/HerWarHerVoice

Her War Her Voice, For the Spouses and loved ones

http://www.facebook.com/LifeAfterWar

Courage Beyond is for the Veterans or families. It's a resource for those who need help

Feeling Suicidal? Alone? Like no one understands? Call
1-866-781-8010

TRAITMARKER personality assessment (TraitMarker is
founded and owned by Robbie Grayson)

http://www.traitmarker.com/
http://www.facebook.com/traitmarker
http://www.facebook.com/TraitmarkerPTSD

ANGELS
IN SADR CITY

A SOLDIER'S MEMOIR ON THE FINAL FIGHT FOR BAGHDAD

ANTHONY FARINA
WITH JOHN REYES

angelsinsadr.com

FROM
WEDDING BELLS
TO HAND GRENADES

What One Army Wife Wished Her Church & Community Knew
About Deployment & the Military Family

A TRAITMARKER
BOOK CLUB
PUBLICATION

NICOLE BROCX LEE

From Wedding Bells to Hand Grenades
(facebook page)

TRIGGERPIECES

THOUGHTS THAT WAR STIRRED UP IN ONE
FEMALE COMBAT VETERAN

A TRAITMARKER
BOOK CLUB
PUBLICATION

CLEO DELONER

deserttodesert.com

VOODOO
IN SADR CITY

A CASE STUDY FOR NON-KINETIC WAR

BOONE CUTLER

Summer 2015
boonecutler.com